BIOLOGY

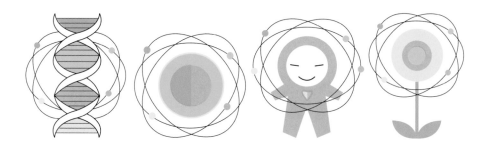

KINGFISHER

NEW YORK

KINGFISHER
LONDON & NEW YORK

Text and design copyright © Toucan Books Ltd. 2008
Based on an original concept by Toucan Books Ltd.
Illustrations copyright © Simon Basher 2008
Published in the United States by Kingfisher,
175 Fifth Ave., New York, NY 10010
Kingfisher is an imprint of Macmillan Children's Books, London.

Consultant: Richard Walker Bsc Phd PGCE

Designed and created by Basher
www.basherbooks.com

3-D body illustrations by Rajeev Doshi at Medi-Mation.
Flower illustration (pages 118, 120) by KJA-artists.

Dedicated to Joyce Theobalds

Distributed in the U.S. by Macmillan, 175 Fifth Ave., New York, NY 10010
Distributed in Canada by H.B. Fenn and Company Ltd., 34 Nixon Road,
Bolton, Ontario L7E 1W2

Library of Congress Cataloging-in-Publication data
has been applied for.

ISBN: 978-0-7534-6622-3

Kingfisher books are available for special promotions and premiums.
For details contact: Special Markets Department, Macmillan,
175 Fifth Avenue, New York, NY 10010.

For more information, please visit www.kingfisherbooks.com

Printed in China
10 9 8 7 6 5 4 3 2 1
1TR/1010/WKT/SCHOY/140MA

CONTENTS

Biology
Introduction

Biology isn't all about skeletons and specimen jars—it's alive and kicking and crawling around in the bushes outside! It is the study of life, taking in the animals, plants, and the stranger creatures of the world, their inner workings as well as the minuscule cells, proteins, and DNA that run them. Life is a strange and marvelous thing. It is also still a big mystery. There could be anywhere between 1.5 and 30 million species of living things on Earth. We know a lot about the big beasts, but we are still in the dark about most creepy-crawlies and microscopic bugs.

Charles Darwin was the man famous for monkeying around with our ideas about biology. He made the most startling of suggestions—that species (things as varied as humans, pigeons, and daffodils) can change with time. It's a dog-eat-dog world out there; it's also a beetle-eat-dung and lion-eat-man world, and only the fittest will survive. Those that are best at surviving when the environment changes live to fight another day. Darwin called this concept natural selection, and it completely changed the way we view the world. Sometimes the simplest ideas are the best!

Charles Darwin

CHAPTER 1
Building Blocks

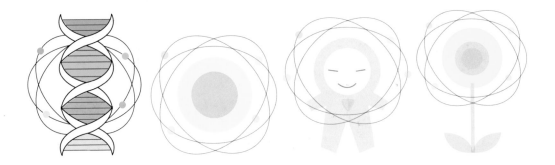

Please don't dismiss this diminutive group of tiny guys—they may be too small to see without a microscope, but they hold the secrets to life itself! They run the inner workings of every living thing on Earth. The leader of the pack is Cell, while the other Building Blocks live inside. Some of the team started out as free agents—for example, billions of years ago, Mitochondria used to live wild as a type of bacteria—but they all now choose to work together within the cell. The brains behind the gang is DNA, who lives in a headquarters called the nucleus. Passing on his genes is the ultimate goal of life.

Cell

Mitochondria

DNA

RNA

Ribosomes

Enzymes

Cell

■ Building Blocks

✳ The smallest living part of a protist, fungus, or animal
✳ Your body is made up entirely of these useful beings
✳ Each cell is a specialist and has a special job to do

You can't help but love me. Every part of your body is made of me—and I'm all yours! I'm totally devoted to you because I couldn't survive on my own. You are a collection of many millions of me and my friends, and I do everything for you—move, eat, think, and feel. If necessary, I will even die for you.

There's nothing gloomy about life inside this cell. I'm a slippery bag with a lot going on within. I buzz with activity, with around 100 million molecules whizzing around inside me. I have a team of chemical workers who manufacture 20,000 different substances, all vital to life. My most amazing stunt is to split in half and make another fully working copy of myself. This is how I construct your body from only a few hundred different types of me.

● Discoverer: Robert Hooke (1665)
● Average size: 2×10^{-5}m
● Number of cells in human body: 100 trillion

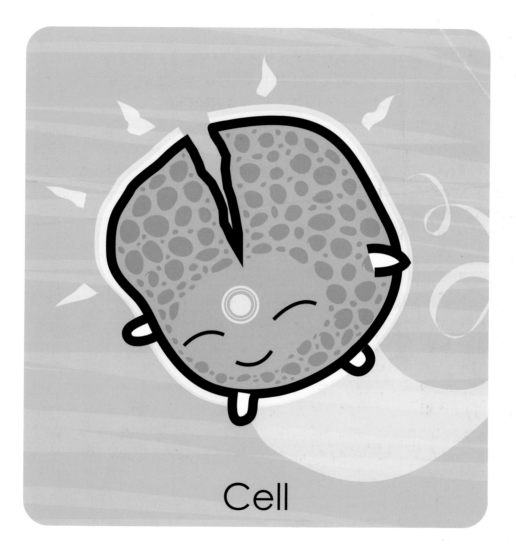

Cell

Mitochondria

■ Building Blocks

✳ Pocket rockets that release all the energy for your body
✳ Tiny power plants working inside every cell
✳ Small hot rods that even carry their own supply of DNA

Lean and mean, we always work at full steam! We are one of Cell's internal machines—his top engineers. We burn food to make a superfuel called ATP. When Cell needs a boost, we smash apart the ATPs, which unleash flashes of life-giving energy. Waste not, want not; we recycle the leftover pieces back into new ATPs.

Shaped like torpedoes, we are visitors to your body. Scientists think that we are bacteria that decided to join Cell's internal management team when animals and plants were first evolving. But we haven't given up our independence completely—we keep our own separate genes, which are passed on via your mother. This means that it's up to us to decide when we divide and grow. When Cell needs to work harder, we boost our numbers.

● Average size: 1×10^{-6} m
● Number of genes per mitochondrion: 37
● ATPs made per second: five million

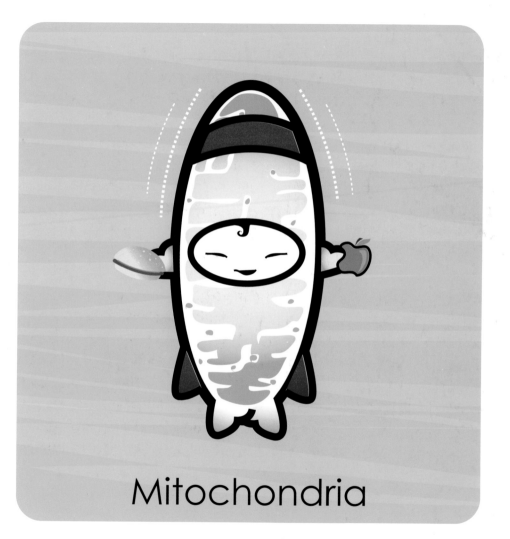

Mitochondria

DNA
■ Building Blocks

❋ A library of info telling your body's cells how to build you
❋ Shaped as a double helix, this chemical spiral codes for life
❋ Full name is deoxyribonucleic acid

Some people think that I'm a totally twisted individual, but while my slinky curves turn heads, I'm actually quite a bookish character. I'm so astounding that within my graceful folds and sinuous switchbacks lies the secret of life itself.

Cell has a library of me, called the genome, stored for safekeeping in the nucleus. The library has 46 "books" in it called chromosomes. Each page of each book is a gene that holds the code for one attribute—your hair color or weakness to certain diseases, for example. The words in these books of life are molecules that link together to make my corkscrew chain. Strangely, most of your DNA is junk—it has no meaning. Although each person's DNA is unique, 99 percent of it is identical to that of everyone else.

● Discoverer: Friedrich Miescher (1869)
● Number of human genes: 20,000 to 25,000
● Number of times the body's DNA is damaged per day: 10,000

DNA

RNA
■ Building Blocks

✳ A shadowy figure who pulls the strings behind the scenes
✳ Built like DNA but without the double twist
✳ Three-letter name means ribonucleic acid

I will always live in the shadow of my dazzling cousin, DNA. It's unfair—DNA gets all the attention for just *holding* the secrets of life. *I'm* the one who does all the work!

I'm much too busy to sit around doing nothing all day like DNA. As one of the few molecules allowed to slip in and out of the nucleus, I can get everywhere. Like a spy selling secrets, I make a copy of DNA's genetic manual and spread it throughout a cell.

I unravel DNA's double helix into two strands and then mold my body to fit with one of them. Then, with the help of Ribosomes, the master code breakers in Cell, I follow the instructions in the manual and make the molecules that the body's workers need.

● Date of discovery: 1939
● Average size: 3.5×10^{-7}m
● Viruses that use RNA: retroviruses such as HIV

RNA

Ribosomes

■ Building Blocks

✻ A cell's protein factories, which follow genetic instructions
✻ Controlled by strands of RNA copied from DNA
✻ Found in all cells, even bacteria

We're the craftworkers who build the proteins that your cells need. We might sound simple, but we are actually very complicated. We do whatever DNA tells us; we're the only guys who can read his ancient genetic code. People often call us protein factories, but we are not large industrial plants. Instead, we are delicate workshops made of twin, interlocking parts.

A protein is a chain of smaller links called amino acids. Each gene in a piece of DNA lists the acids in the correct order to make a particular protein. We assemble the sections of each protein on a production line, following the orders of RNA, who's been sent from the nucleus with a copy of a gene. Proteins are useful things. Our products might become muscles, enzymes, or hormones.

● Discoverer: George Palade (1950s)
● Size: 25×10^{-9}m
● Number per cell: approximately 15,000

Ribosomes

Enzymes
■ Building Blocks

* ✳ Protein machines that run your metabolism
* ✳ Used in digestion to break down food into simple chemicals
* ✳ There are 2,709 different types working in the human body

We are the body's construction workers. Some of us build things up, while the rest of us form a wrecking crew, stripping down everything to its raw materials. We are on duty throughout the body. Most of us work inside Cell, but we also do important work in Stomach. We are even mixed in with saliva to help the teeth soften food.

We don't like to get our hands dirty, but we make chemical reactions happen without getting involved ourselves. We're made from twisted proteins, and each of us has a certain shape. We are locks that only particular key molecules will fit. Once each type of molecule is fitted into place, we work our magic and new substances are formed. Our shapes depend on how we are put together. A blueprint of each of us is stored in DNA's genome.

* ● Thrombin: enzyme used to help blood clot, forming a scab over a cut
* ● Amylase: enzyme that digests the starch in potatoes or bread
* ● In industry: used to make cheese and beer and added to laundry detergent

Enzymes

CHAPTER 2
Life

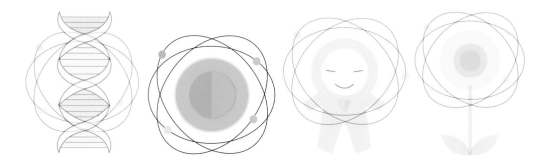

From the tiniest microscopic bacteria to gigantic, towering pine trees, this gang is simply bursting with life! But despite the mind-boggling variety of this mob, they all do the same "life" things such as getting food, using energy, building bodies, and making new versions of themselves. Scientists have spent hundreds of years describing life. The biology brainiacs have discovered that there are five basic types of living things, so they group them into five huge collections, called kingdoms. The kingdoms are: animals, plants, fungi, bacteria, and other tiny creatures called protists.

Virus
■ Life

✳ Rogue package of DNA or RNA that invades cells
✳ One of the smallest living things there is
✳ Responsible for many illnesses, including the common cold

I'm an itty-bitty stalker who doles out large helpings of doom. I'm a death-dealing devil and real bad news for all other living things. Sometimes I'm just a nuisance— such as when I cause a cold, the chickenpox, cold sores, or a quite messy vomiting sickness. But I can also be deadly. My dangerous forms include influenza, measles, and HIV. I'm the worst kind of guest—I bust right into your body, hijack Cell, and make him my slave.

I'm a tiny bandit of DNA or RNA in a protein coating. I couldn't be simpler; I barely count as a living thing. I don't eat or grow and I can't reproduce by myself. So I make Cell do it for me. I have a chemical disguise that makes me look like a friend, not a foe. Luckily for you, T Cell and the rest of the immune system are there to drive me away.

● Size: 25 to 300 x 10^{-9}m
● Number of known viruses: 5,000
● Officially extinct virus: smallpox

Virus

Bacteria

■ Life

☀ Tiny single-celled organisms that live almost everywhere
☀ Some of the world's worst diseases are caused by bacteria
☀ These minuscule guys have been around for 3.5 billion years

Our motto is "simplicity equals success." Since the dawn of life, we've done very well by not being bothered about complexity. We are tiny sacks of chemicals with none of the machinery that other types of cells have, just enough to get by. We are everywhere—literally. We hang out in rocks buried 2 mi. (3km) underground, chill out in nuclear waste tanks, live in boiling mud, and can even survive being released into outer space! To us, a dash of bleach and warm water is more dangerous than anything else.

We may be invisible, but the world couldn't live without us. We recycle all waste and make the soil fertile, and we pump out just as much oxygen as trees do. Intestines carry 2.2 lbs. (1kg) of us, and one trillion of us are grazing away on Skin—more than there are people on Earth.

● Total weight of all bacteria: 150 times the total weight of all humans
● Reproductive rate: up to 28,000 copies in one day
● Bacterial diseases include: cholera, plague, tuberculosis

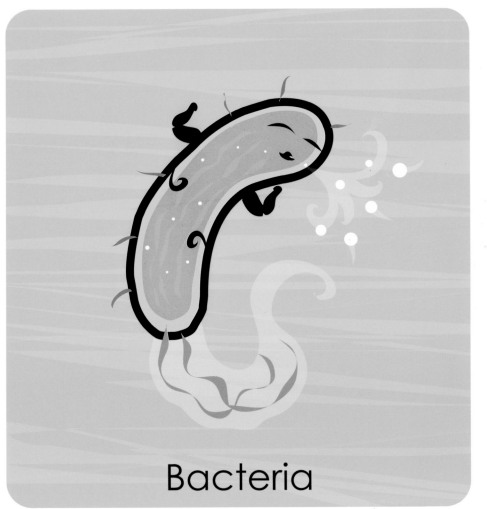

Bacteria

Protists

■ Life

✳ Living things whose bodies are made from a single cell
✳ Mostly, these guys are hundreds of times larger than bacteria
✳ Neither plants nor animals but something in between

We are the ancient ones. Billions of years ago, some of us joined together to become the first plants, animals, and fungi. But most of us just want to be alone. We use most of the same equipment as animal and plant cells, such as Mitochondria and Ribosomes, but all we need to survive is a single cell—not a complicated body. But don't get us confused with Bacteria!

We go by many names: amoebas, algae, or protozoans. Some of us live like plants, using sunlight to make food; others are hunters that chase Bacteria through the slime before spearing them with barbed darts. Some of us even do both! We move in mysterious ways, too—propelled by a corkscrew tail, pushed by hairlike cilia, or simply by folding our bodies along in one direction.

● Average size: 0.0004 to 0.02 in. (0.01 to 0.5mm)
● Deadliest protists: *Plasmodium* (malaria—causes one million deaths per year)
● Other diseases caused by protists: sleeping sickness, dysentery

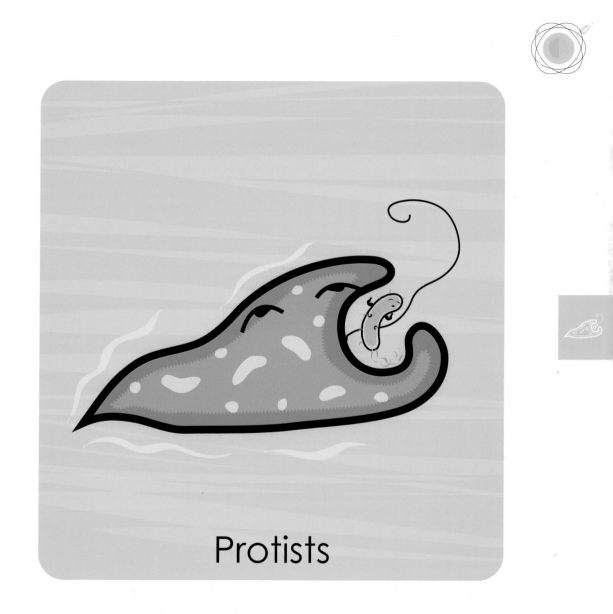

Protists

Fungus

■ Life

✳ A member of a rotten buch that includes mushrooms, molds, and yeasts
✳ Can be huge, spreading under ground for miles
✳ Used to make the best antibiotic medicines, such as penicillin

I know I'm often a little yucky, but don't forget about me—I have a kingdom of my own. Even so, I am the poor relative of plants and animals. You give me horrible names like dead man's fingers, death cup, and stinkhorn. Of course, that might be because I can be deadly when eaten.

You are most likely to see me in a damp forest, where I send toadstools and mushrooms out into the open. But that's just the tip of the iceberg. Mostly I'm made from a mass of wispy threads that are hidden from view. And I like to spread out, sometimes covering a huge area.

I am nature's cleaner. I love dead bodies and any pieces of rotting waste. I slowly devour it all, gradually turning it into sticky mush until there is nothing left.

● Foods made with fungi: blue cheese, beer, bread
● Largest fungus: honey mushroom, Oregon (97 million sq. ft./9 million m^2)
● Fungal diseases include: athlete's foot, ringworm

Fungus

Seedless Plants
■ Life

☀ Ancient plants that spread to new areas using spores
☀ Include ferns, mosses, and seaweeds
☀ The first types of plants to live on land

We are the ugly brothers and sisters of the plant kingdom. All of us use Chlorophyll to make food from sunlight. But we don't have anything as pretty as Flower or as tasty as Fruit. Some of us don't even have Leaf or Root!

We are a bunch of many types of ancient plants. Some of us do like to live near the shore. It's not all sun and surf for seaweeds, though, as they cope with being dried out and then soaked through again twice each day! Mosses and their buddies, liverworts, were the first land plants around 475 million years ago. But 175 million years later, forests of tree ferns also covered the land. Our breeding process is quite complicated. Unlike Flowering Plants, we breed using a sperm and an egg, not pollen. Instead of seeds, we spread spores that grow into new plants.

● Largest fronds (fern leaves): king fern (30 ft./9m long)
● Fastest-growing seaweed: giant kelp (3.3 ft./1m per day)
● Edible seaweeds: laver, Irish moss, agar

Seedless Plants

Conifers
■ Life

✳ Evergreen trees that are the longest-living things on Earth
✳ Small needle-shaped leaves can survive in icy weather
✳ 550 species of conifers include pines, firs, and spruces

We are the biggest, toughest, and longest-living plants. For many, we are the symbol of Christmas, and we "spruce" up the holiday season. While many Flowering Plants spend the winter looking leafless and lifeless, we keep our needle-shaped leaves all year long. Even a blizzard won't get us down—our smooth diagonal sides form chutes so that the heavy snow falls off. Our fast-growing trunks can be cut into planks, and our wood can be pulped to make paper.

We tough it out in extreme cold, poor soil, and on high, windswept mountains. Our spiky leaves are tough and waxy, so they don't dry out or freeze easily. Few animals can stomach them either. But our cones make us who we are. We invented Seed around 300 million years ago and store him inside our cones.

● Tallest conifer: coast redwood (378 ft./115.2m)
● Thickest trunk: Montezuma cypress (37.5 ft./11.42m diameter)
● Oldest conifer: Great Basin bristlecone pine (4,700 years old)

Conifers

Flowering Plants
■ Life

✳ Showoffs who bring flowers, pollen, and fruit into the world
✳ Many scented and colorful plants are lifelong pals with insects
✳ For 130 million years, they have been the main plants on Earth

Before we came on the scene, the world must have been a dull place. Conifers are so stern and stiff (and they all look so similar), and Seedless Plants are all dressed in drab greens and browns. We are fabulous—real stunners—and bring color to Earth.

We are very image conscious. Our flowers' arrangements of color and scent attract animals. We want them to pay us a visit so that we can get them to carry Pollen to our neighbors. But some of us, such as grass, are content to bend with the wind, which spreads Pollen just as well. We are also important to humans. A lot of your food comes from us—wheat and rice, corn and oats, most vegetables, peas and beans, oils, fruit, and nuts. We even provide the cotton fibers for your clothes.

● Scientific name: angiosperms
● Earliest known flower: *Archaefructus liaoningensis* (125 million years ago)
● Largest flowering plant: *Eucalyptus amygdalina* (410 ft./125m)

Flowering Plants

Invertebrates
■ Life

* Animals without backbones, who colonized land first
* The first animals to evolve, at least 650 million years ago
* Include the world's tiniest creatures but some monsters, too

Although you might think of us as spineless simpletons, we rule the world. Get over yourselves, you big-boned blunderers—we make up 97 percent of all animal species on Earth!

We include everything from tiny plankton floating in the sea to giant squids, the original sea monsters that are longer than most boats. In between are all sorts of soft jellyfish and slimy worms. Some of us, such as clams and starfish, are hard cases who are holed up inside shells—for life! Our largest group is the armor-plated Arthropods.

For our size, we beat most vertebrates hands down—even though we don't have any hands, of course. We include world-beating jumpers and weightlifters, and we hold the world land-speed record, too. Top that!

● Highest jumper: spittlebug (can jump 70 times its height)
● Best weightlifter: rhinoceros beetle (can lift 850 times its weight)
● Fastest runner: American cockroach (can run 50 times its own length per second)

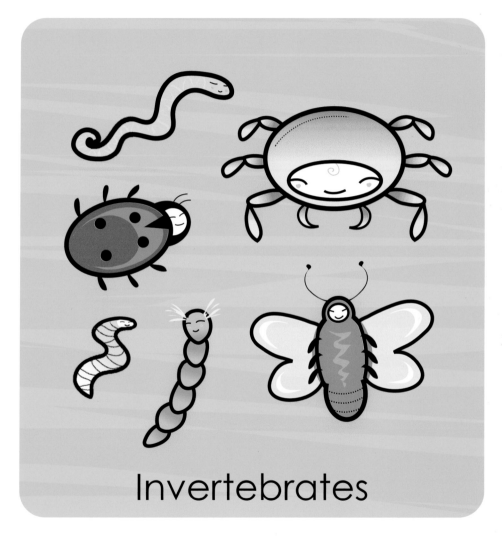

Invertebrates

Jellies
■ Life

✷ Brainless wonders with circular bodies and trailing tentacles
✷ Food and waste come in and out through the same hole
✷ Include jellyfish, sea anemones, and corals

We're 98 percent water, but we're no drips! We may be almost invisible, but some of us have a sting in our tails. Your best chance of seeing us is when we crowd together in a bloom. In the darkness of the deep sea, we put on light shows, too. Some of us choose settled lives. Billions of corals huddle together, forming huge reefs. Some are even visible from outer space.

Jellies

● Deadliest jelly: box jellyfish
● Largest jelly: lion's mane jellyfish (6.5 ft./2m wide
● Number of species: 9,000

* ☀ Include leeches, terrifying tapeworms, and grimy earthworms
* ☀ Divided into segmented worms, roundworms, and flatworms
* ☀ At least 55,000 species, and they're all completely legless

Worms

Let's face it—we can't afford to be fussy. We're happy to live almost anywhere. With no backbones for support, we grow our largest in the water, but we also wiggle through the soil, of course. If you are very unlucky, we might be crawling inside your blood or intestines. We are found in other inhospitable places, too, even hot water belched from seabed volcanoes!

* ● Longest worm: nemertean (164 ft./50m)
* ● Number of earthworms: up to 50 per square foot of soil (500/m²)
* ● Number of segments in an earthworm: 150

Arthropods
■ Life

❉ Creepy-crawlies with skeletons on the outside, not the inside
❉ Include insects, spiders, scorpions, and crabby crustaceans
❉ Evolved in the ocean before becoming the first land animals

Welcome to the age of the arthropod! More than 84 percent of all animals on this planet belong to our mind-boggling collection of invertebrates. We evolved from worms somewhere out there on the seabed more than 500 million years ago. Our name means "jointed legs," and we have many. Most of us are insects with a measly six limbs, but scuttling millipedes have 200 or more!

We all have bodies formed in sections. Unlike vertebrates, which hang their squishy parts on an internal skeleton, we keep our soft parts safe in a suit of armor called an exoskeleton. Our feelers do a lot more than just feel— some of us use them to smell, too. We see the world differently from you. Spiders, for example, have eyes in the backs of their heads!

● Edible arthropods include: shrimp, lobsters, crabs
● Largest arthropod: spider crab (14 lbs./6.4kg, 12.5 ft./3.8m across)
● Smallest arthropod: *Eriophyid* mite (0.006 in./0.15mm)

Arthropods

Insects
■ Life

* ✹ Six-legged arthropods that are found almost everywhere
* ✹ Three fourths of all known animal species are insects
* ✹ More than one million types have been found—and still counting!

We are the biggest gang of Arthropods. Insects rule! We are masters of the air and land. The salty ocean waves are the only places we don't thrive, but we're working on it!

There is a lot more to us than buzzy wasps that spoil a picnic or vibrant butterflies that flit around a garden. Many of us are hidden from view: beetles are toiling in the soil, busy ants are laboring under the ground, and cockroaches are getting dirty in garbage dumps.

One of the secrets of our success is that our kids don't get in the way. Most insect young spend their days as wormlike grubs, maggots, and caterpillars. These larvae do nothing but eat and grow. Then it's time to transform into glorious adults, and the race is on to find mates.

* ● Heaviest insect: giant weta (2.5 oz./70g)
* ● Estimated number of undiscovered insect species: 30 million
* ● Deadliest insects: mosquitoes carrying malaria

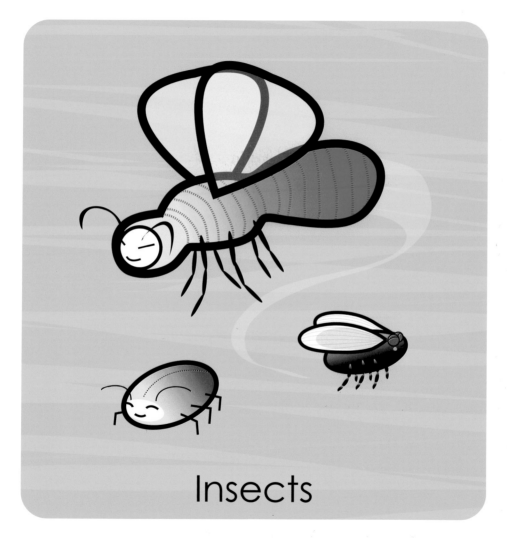

Insects

Mollusks

■ Life

* Around 128,000 species who mostly live in the ocean
* Slugs and snails are the only land-going mollusks
* Many mollusks carry their protective shell houses with them

We do our best to look like tough hard cases, but inside we're real softies. It's not always obvious that we are related—we've got snails, oysters, clams, and mussels in our clan. Some of us sift food from the water with a slimy net; the rest of us scrape up food with a jagged cutting tool called a radula. The largest (and most intelligent) mollusks of all are octopuses and squids.

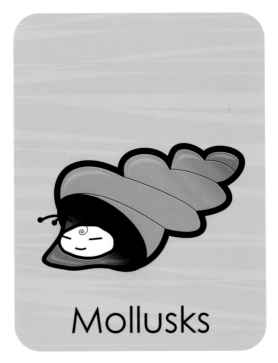

Mollusks

● Largest mollusk: colossal squid (46 ft./14m)
● Deadliest mollusk: blue-ringed octopus
● Largest shellfish: giant clam (53 in./137cm)

* A prickly bunch with skeletons made of calcium, a little like bone
* Adults move using a system of water pumps that power tubular feet
* Babies swim freely in the water; adults are normally seabed bound

Starfish

Excuse us, darling, VIPs coming through! We're the stars of the sea. Our many arms drip with jewel-like spines, and we bring color to the drab rocks and sand on the seabed. We are pretty special. We can change color and will grow a new arm if an annoying snapper breaks one off. Other members of the family include unruly spiked sea urchins and bland sea cucumbers.

● Largest number of arms: *Helicoilaster* (50)
● Heaviest starfish: *Thromidia catalai* (13 lbs./6kg)
● Poisonous starfish: crown-of-thorns

Fish
■ Life

※ The largest group of vertebrates, with around 25,000 species
※ A wet bunch that breathes under water using gills
※ Many food fish are in danger from greedy overfishing

When we arrived on the scene 500 million years ago, we caused a splash! We were the first animals with backbones, and we've been braving the water ever since.

We range from the deep oceans to rivers and flooded caves. We are the world's top swim team—most of us have an air (swim) bladder to keep us afloat. We don't have legs, just fins, but a few of us can flip-flop around on land, and some can even fly!

Most of us have skeletons made from tiny, sharp bones. Watch out—they might get stuck in your throat. But one notorious gang of fierce fish—led by the sharks—is completely boneless. These fish have rubbery cartilage instead. Be careful that you don't get stuck in *their* throats!

● Fastest fish: sailfish (600 mph/100km/h)
● Longest-living fish: beluga sturgeon (more than 100 years)
● Largest fish: whale shark (25 tons)

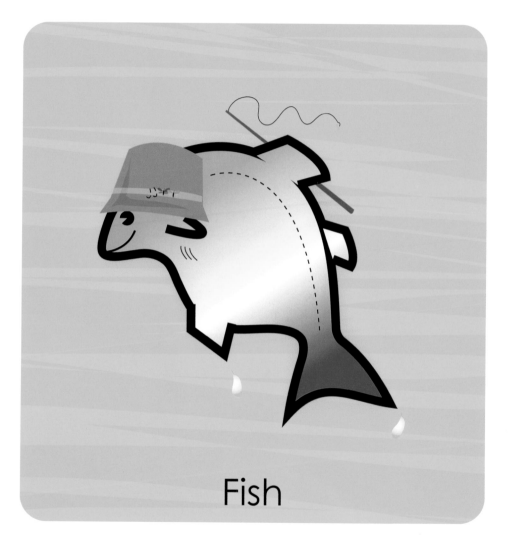

Fish

Amphibians
■ Life

☀ Bulging-eyed slimeballs that live near water
☀ Of the 6,000 species, most are frogs and toads
☀ Thin-skinned and cold-blooded, many are poisonous

We are a group of secretive, sun-shy creatures. Take some time to get to know us and you'll love us, warts and all! As well as leaping frogs and waddling toads, we include salamanders, newts, and blind, legless creatures called caecilians. We live in damp places because we breathe through our skin and need to keep it moist and fresh.

We were the first vertebrates to try life on land, 400 million years ago. Since then, we've been commuting between land and water. Some of us never leave the water even now, and our fishy past is there for all to see in the jelly-covered eggs that we lay, always in or close to the water. Our babies are born with gills and spend their childhoods in the water. Once we've developed lungs, we can hunt on land. Watch out, Insects. Here we come!

● Largest frog: Goliath frog (12 in./30cm; weighs as much as a pet cat)
● Longest leap: tree frogs can jump 20 times their own length
● Most poisonous frog: golden poison-arrow frog

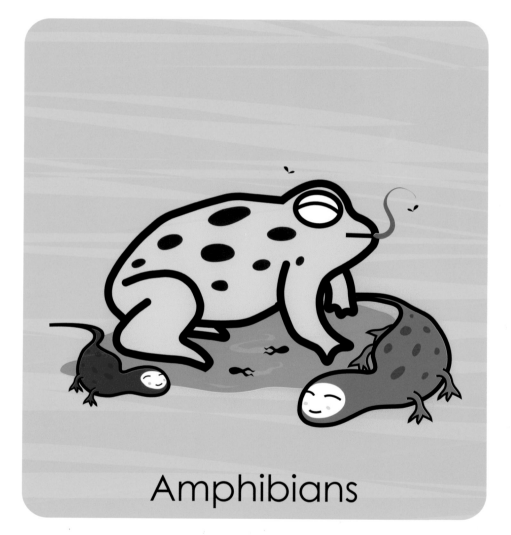

Amphibians

Reptiles
■ Life

* ✳ 7,700 species include turtles, crocodiles, lizards, and snakes
* ✳ A bunch of sun worshipers with dry, scaly skin
* ✳ Most young hatch from eggs with soft but waterproof shells

We're most likely to be found lying in the sunshine. There's nothing we love better than soaking up some rays. We're not at our best in the morning—our cold blood means that we're sluggish starters, and we have to wait to warm up before we can get down to the day's business. But we can afford to sleep in—we need to eat only around one fifth as much as the hot-bodied Mammals and Birds to keep our bodies in working order.

We might look lazy, but don't be fooled—we have a long history. Way back when, our dinosaur cousins ruled the world. Perhaps our glory days are over—but some of us are still at the top of our game: you'll know what we mean if you ever come eye to eye with a grinning crocodile or meet a death-dealing cobra with syringelike fangs.

* ● Largest reptile: saltwater crocodile (more than 20 ft./6m)
* ● Smallest reptile: dwarf sphaero gecko (0.64 in./16mm)
* ● Longest-living reptile: giant tortoise (more than 170 years)

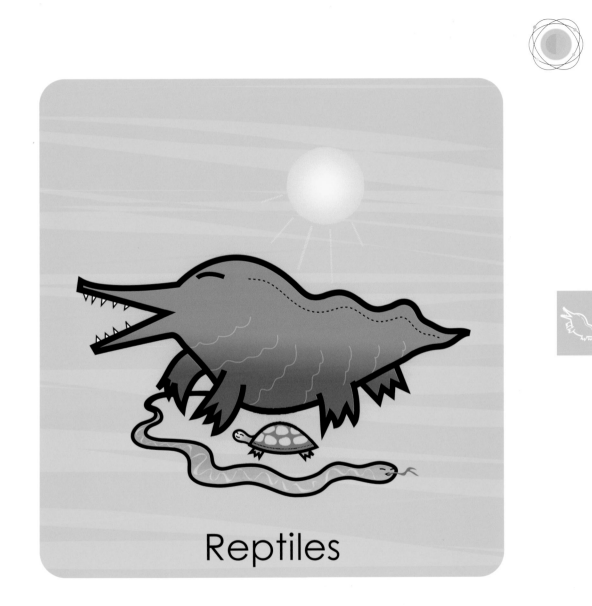

Reptiles

51

Birds
■ Life

* 10,000 species of flying experts that evolved from dinosaurs
* Feathered friends that lay tough-shelled eggs
* Colorful twitterers that fill the world with song

Ever wished you could fly? In your dreams! We soar effortlessly through the air while you earthlings stay rooted to the ground. The sky's the limit for us fly guys! We're all built to the same template—two legs, two wings, waterproof feathers, and warm blood. We need to keep our weight down and have hollow bones filled with air and horny beaks instead of heavy teeth. Our beaks are shaped according to the food we eat, but without gnashers, we need help to chop up our meals. That's why you'll often find us pecking around for grit—it grinds up the food in our churning bellies.

We like crowds and sometimes flock together in the hundreds of thousands. Many of us take a winter vacation every year, flying off to sunnier lands to escape the cold.

● Fastest flier: eider duck (170 mph/270km/h)
● Smallest bird: bee hummingbird (2 in./5cm)
● Highest flier: Ruppell's gryphon vulture (36,000 ft./11,000m)

Birds

Mammals

■ Life

✳ Fur-covered animals that feed their babies milk
✳ Almost one half of the 4,600 species are rats and other rodents
✳ The world's most famous mammal is reading this book now!

We're the top dogs of the animal kingdom—and the top cats, skunks, and llamas, too. Over the past 60 million years or so, we've made this little planet our own—we can survive more or less everywhere besides the icy wastelands of Antarctica and the deepest ocean floors.

You couldn't find a more diverse bunch of beasts than us. We are both the hunters and the hunted, often fighting with tooth and claw. We are bears and bats, dolphins and deep-diving whales, tiny mice and enormous elephants, kangaroos, cows, and kooky duck-billed platypuses. But we have more in common than just our hair. Our kids are born live (except for two or three weirdo egg-laying types called monotremes), and our first meals are always drinks of warm milk straight from our mother.

● Fastest mammal: cheetah (60 mph/95km/h over 1,640 ft./500m)
● Largest mammal: blue whale (190 tons)
● Poisonous mammals: duck-billed platypus, solenodon, water shrew

Mammals

CHAPTER 3
Body Parts

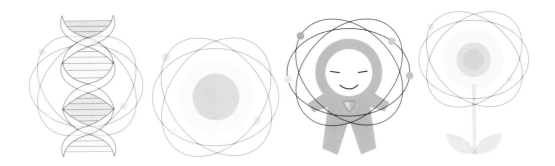

This crew of hard-working, heavy-duty guys runs the body. They are an all-star gang who make up YOU—one of the most complex organisms that inhabits the planet. Every single member of this team is an expert with a certain area of responsibility. Some are part of a body system that controls one function of the body such as moving, eating, or getting rid of waste. Others are organs—fleshy factories that make or collect the things that the body needs in order to survive. And they are all made from trillions of individual cells. There are almost seven billion people on Earth, and all of them are made the same way—just like you!

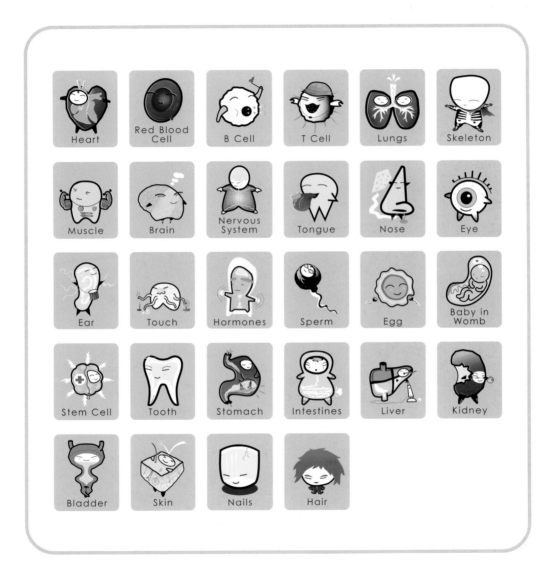

Heart

■ Body Parts

* A fist-size organ that pumps blood around your body
* This tireless muscleman sits just to the left in your chest
* When this guy gets sick, the rest of the body can't keep going

I'm a pounding muscle beating at the core of your existence. I am officially your body's hardest-working part. I pump 2,100 gal. (8,000L) of blood every day. And I never stop or get tired.

If I do stop beating, you're in trouble. Brain can only survive for a few minutes without the life-giving oxygen that I pump throughout the body. My double-pump system sends blood to Lungs first, to power up on oxygen, and then it returns to me and I send it shooting around the body to Cell and his friends. The pressure I generate in your arteries is enough to squirt blood across the room. But I'm a sensitive guy—when you get scared or nervous, I beat faster. I also make you blush by pumping blood into Skin.

That's me!

● Adult heart rate: 75 beats per minute
● Blood pumped in one year: 793,000 gal. (3 million L)
● Number of heartbeats in a lifetime: 1 to 3 billion

Heart

Red Blood Cell

■ Body Parts

- ✳ Live-fast-die-young hero who gives blood its red color
- ✳ A round cell with no nucleus, but full of iron
- ✳ Busy fellow who carries oxygen around the body

I'm a breath of fresh air for your body. I'm a specialist, trained for only one thing—to bring life-giving oxygen to Cell whenever and wherever he needs it.

I use an iron-rich chemical called hemoglobin to pick up the oxygen from Lungs. When I'm full of oxygen, I am bright scarlet. When the blood is full of carbon-dioxide waste thrown out by Cell, I appear much darker.

Just one drop of blood has around five million of me in it, so imagine how many there are in the 1.3 gal. (5L) that pump around your body. I'm made in the marrow inside bones, which pumps out two million new versions of me every second. When I'm old, Liver will break me down, and my red color will end up as the "yellow" in urine.

- ● Discoverer: Jan Swammerdam (1658)
- ● Average size: 7×10^{-6}m
- ● Average life span: four months

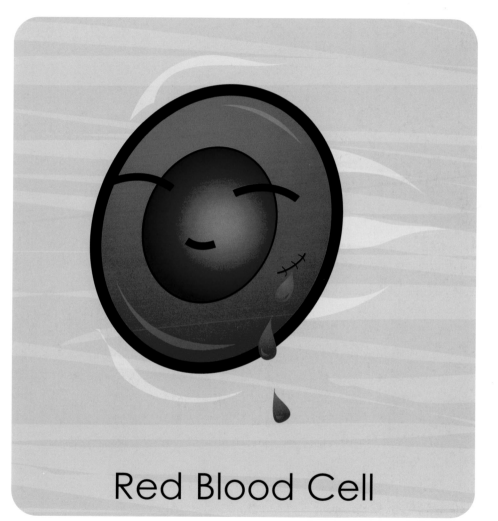

Red Blood Cell

B Cell
■ Body Parts

* ☀ A white blood cell that protects you from future invasions
* ☀ Patrols the blood and lymphatic systems looking for trouble
* ☀ Highlights dangerous invaders with markers called antibodies

I am your body's police officer. I watch out for trouble and raise the alarm when dangerous invaders appear. I can remember what they all look like from the last time they made you sick. But I make sure you won't get fooled again. I release chemical flags that plant themselves on the invaders. Tough T Cell knows just what my markers mean: "Kill this now!"

B Cell

* ● B stands for: bursa of Fabricius
* ● Other name: B lymphocyte
* ● Cancer of the B cells: lymphoma

T Cell

Body Parts

* A white blood cell that works in the immune system
* A member of your body's special forces, trained to kill invaders
* Does battle in the lymphatic system and in blood

T Cell

I'm a natural-born killer. I cruise around your body's blood vessels looking for nasty invaders such as Bacteria and Virus. When you get sick, there can be as many as 7,000 of me in one drop of blood. My weapons are designed to kill a certain invader such as the flu virus. B Cell guides me to the right target. When the trouble is over, I am deactivated in order to stop me from causing havoc.

- *T* stands for: thymus
- Other name: T lymphocyte
- Disease of the T cells: HIV (AIDS) attacks them

Lungs
■ Body Parts

* A pair of gas bags that are located on both sides of your chest
* Spongy lobes that suck in oxygen and breathe out waste gas
* Total surface area inside is as large as a tennis court

We are a set of beautiful twins that give your body a good airing. Life's a gas for us—we take oxygen from the air and pass it to Red Blood Cell. At the same time, we get rid of suffocating carbon-dioxide waste.

We suck air in with the help of a muscular pump called the diaphragm, which rises and falls on top of Liver and Intestines. On the way in, Nose and the throat clean and moisten the air. Once inside, the air rushes into sacs called alveoli. There are 300 million of them inside us, each one covered in tiny blood vessels. This is where we make the switch: oxygen in and carbon dioxide out. We're made of pink foamy flesh, but if you smoke, you'll make us a sooty mess, turning a softly purring machine into wheezing windbags.

Here we are!

● Average capacity: 1.3 gal. (5L)
● Length of lung's airways: 1,500 mi. (2,400km)
● Resting breathing rate: 15 times per minute

Lungs

Skeleton

■ Body Parts

☀ A super group of 206 bones
☀ These upright guys provide a framework for your body
☀ The longest bones are in your legs; the smallest are in your ears

I am the body's supertough hard case, and it's my job to protect and support. I am the superstructure where the rest of the body parts hang out—without me, you'd be nothing more than a floppy pile of flesh.

My bones are stronger than steel and can carry five times my own weight. I achieve this with a special mixture of flexible collagen fibers and the rock-hard mineral calcium phosphate. Ties called ligaments join my bones together. I can crack from time to time, but I can also repair myself with my powers of regeneration.

Like Italian cannelloni pasta, my bones are hollow and filled with mush. It's called marrow. This stuff makes 175 billion new red blood cells per day.

All 206 bones are in here! ➤

● Total weight of skeleton: around 20 lbs. (9kg)
● Person with the most broken bones: Evel Knievel (35 fractures)
● Number of bones in spine: 26

Skeleton

Muscle

■ Body Parts

- ❋ The muscleman who keeps your body on the move
- ❋ A bundle of protein filaments that shorten when electrified
- ❋ Meat is the muscle of animals such as cows and chickens

Skeleton always tries to take the credit for keeping you upright, but without me, all he can do is stand still. That bag of old bones just provides anchor points for me and the 649 other muscles to do the body's real work.

Once I've gotten my instructions from Nervous System, I work by contracting tiny bundles of fibers so that they get shorter and fatter. I can only pull, not push, so I often work in pairs to tug Skeleton's lazy bones around. For example, your biceps bend your arm at the elbow and your triceps, on the other side of the bone, straighten it.

Skeletal muscles do the moving and lifting work. Smooth muscles are automatic and power Bladder and Intestines. Heart's muscles never get tired!

I'm everywhere!

- ● Largest muscle: gluteus maximus (buttocks)
- ● Number of muscles needed to smile: 12
- ● Number of muscles needed to frown: 11

Muscle

Brain
Body Parts

☀ This clever character controls all of your body's processes
☀ A softy made of electrified gray matter and white matter
☀ The location of the mind, where you do your thinking

It's a no-brainer: I am the body's most important organ. All the body crew claim that they are indispensable, but I'm the only one you can't replace. I control you. Remove your hardhat—the skull—and underneath you will find a juicy, wrinkly blob. Your hind- and midbrain, at the back, control automatic stuff like breathing and balance.

The forebrain is a whirl of activity that makes you a fully functioning individual. This part of me lets you talk, have harebrained ideas, and laugh at jokes. The information from your five senses is processed here. On good days, I'm also capable of some independent thought, too! All this brainwork needs a lot of resources. I use up one fifth of the oxygen taken in by Lungs, and I have my own dedicated blood supply.

I'm here!

● Number of nerve cells: 100 billion
● Number of connections with each cell: between 10 and 10,000
● Average weight: 3.1 lbs. (1.4kg)

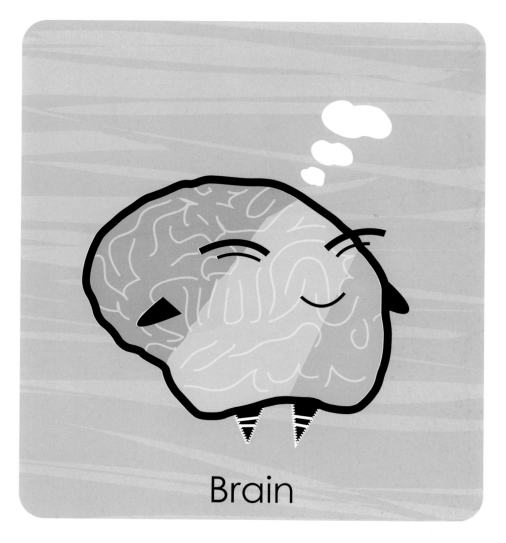

Brain

Nervous System

Body Parts

- ☀ A sensitive guy who feels your pain
- ☀ A live wire who does things without thinking
- ☀ A whole-body network that reacts like greased lightning

I'm a sparky character. I am your communication network, filled with signals of electric pulses. I connect your early-warning system to Brain and then carry his commands to Muscle—in case you need to make a quick getaway.

My billions of branches cover the entire surface of your body with sensitive nerve endings that detect touch, pain, and heat. I also carry messages from your team of detectors—Eye, Ear, Nose, and Tongue—to Brain.

Most of my branches lead back to the spinal cord, which is the body's central information cable. Brain does all the thinking, but reflex actions, like flinching away from a hot surface, are controlled by the cord alone.

I run right through you!

- ● Total length of nerves: 93,000 mi. (150,000km)
- ● Speed of nerve signal: 394 ft. (120m) per second
- ● Voltage of nerve signal: 30mV

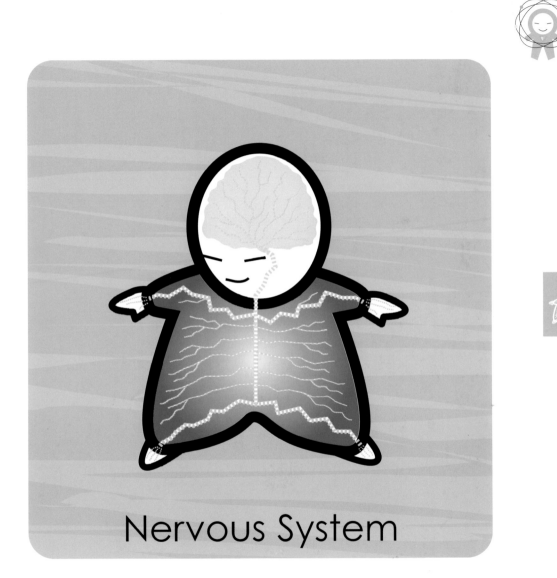

Nervous System

Tongue
■ Body Parts

✳ Sensitive buds on the tongue pick up chemicals in your food
✳ Used to figure out whether food is dangerous or full of nutrients
✳ Powerful tongue muscles can't be beaten for strength

I am the center of operations for your sense of taste. And I'm not a pretty sight—to an outsider, I am a slobbery, drooling wiggler covered in stinky bacteria, but I think I'm made in the best possible taste.

I'm not just used for sloshing food around between the teeth, although my furry surface helps me grip even the gooiest of snacks. I'm also a star player on the speech team—without me, they'd be in trouble. But my pride and joy are the thousands of little lumps that run from my tip, down my sides, and around my back. These buds handle simple tastes like sweet, sour, salty, and bitter, as well as a lesser-known fifth taste called umami, or "meatiness." But I'm no expert compared to Nose. Normally, he checks out food first.

● Longest human tongue: 3.7 in. (9.5cm) from lips to tip when stuck out of mouth
● Life span of taste buds: ten days
● Scientific name for taste: gustation

Tongue

Nose

■ Body Parts

☀ This sensitive fellow runs a chemical-detection system
☀ Has a hairlike lining that sniffs out smells
☀ Scientists refer to the sense of smell as olfaction

I sometimes look down at things, but that is the only way I know how to work. You'd be advised to follow me. I use chemical sensors deep inside me to pluck scents from the air. People rely on sight so much that I often get overlooked, but smell is one of your strongest senses. I'm 10,000 times more sensitive than brutish Tongue. I get you licking your lips before you even realize you're hungry.

My odor detectives are hair-shaped cilia that line chambers inside me. Each cilium watches out for certain chemicals swirling around in the air that you breathe and then sends a signal to Brain. The cilia are sensitive souls—think of that the next time you go rooting around inside me with a finger! Cilia like being damp, but a snotty cold swamps them with mucus, so they barely work at all.

● Sensitivity of nose: can detect 10,000 different smells
● Wind speed of a sneeze: 100 mph (163km/h)
● Size of the cilia zone: 0.40 sq. in. (2.5cm^2)

Nose

Eye
■ Body Parts

※ A squishy light sensor that brings things into focus
※ Inner lining is sensitive to different light frequencies
※ Sight is controlled by the visual cortex at the back of the brain

I'm a true visionary—a mushy ball of clear gel that is your window on the world. I'm used for sight, the principal sense for most people. Gaze deeply into me and you will discover just how complex I really am.

My most appealing feature is my beautiful iris. This colored muscle controls the amount of light that gets inside— otherwise, I might get dazzled. Behind the iris is a flexible friend, the lens. Pulled into shape by Muscle, the lens focuses light beams onto my back wall, or retina. The retina is teeming with cells called rods and cones. Cones detect colors but work only in bright light. The rods are sensitive enough to see in the dark, but they can only pick up black and white. I actually see everything upside down, but clever Brain soon flips it the right way up again.

● Number of rods: 120 million
● Number of cones: seven million
● Purpose of eyelids: wipe eyes clean and keep them moist

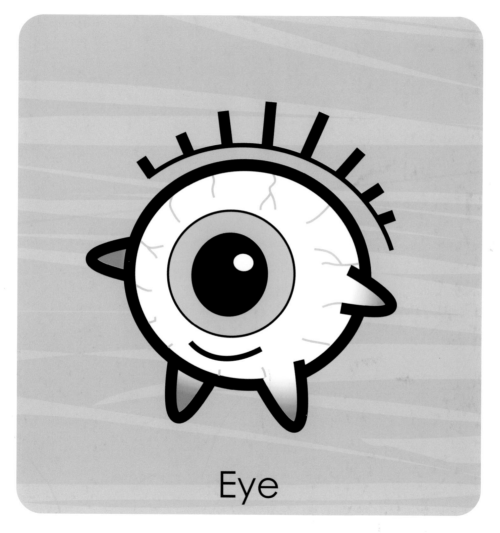

Eye

Ear
■ Body Parts

✳ A funnel-shaped guy that collects sound waves
✳ Sound waves are converted into electric pulses inside
✳ Also used to help you stay balanced

I am your body's hi-fi system—a finely tuned sensor that picks up the tiniest vibrations in the air. Thanks to me, you experience these vibrations as sweet sounds.

My outer section channels airwaves into your ear hole—and then the real business begins. The air beats on a drum of skin, and the rhythm is passed through a group of tiny bones to a shell-shaped structure called the cochlea. The cochlea is full of fluid. Every beat sends a ripple through the fluid, which is picked up by microscopic hairs. The hairs are connected to Nervous System, who carries a signal to Brain. He'll let you know if I hear anything interesting. I'm also well balanced—the inner ear has chambers of jelly that detect changes in body position and give you a sense of what's up and down.

● Length of smallest ear bone (stirrup): 0.12 in. (3mm)
● Speed of sound waves: 1,090 ft. (332m) per second
● Adult ear's sensitivity: 20 to 20,000 hertz

Ear

Touch

■ Body Parts

- ✳ A touchy-feely sense who can also be a real pain!
- ✳ Uses nerve endings in the skin to sense pressure and temperature
- ✳ The most touch-sensitive places are fingertips and lips

Give me a hug—I'm the forgotten sense. I'm at work on every inch of your body and often get overlooked. But I have so many skills—I can feel hot and cold and a whole range of pushes, pinches, and pinpricks. However, I sometimes get even—when I'm feeling itchy, you can't think about anything but me!

I'm right under your skin, where the nerves are plugged into sensors. Tiny hairs in Skin detect the slightest brush or breeze. Another detector looks out for heat, while a separate type feels the cold. Deeper down, nerve endings detect pressure. If my system gets overloaded, I'll send out pulses of pain to warn you of danger. My fabulous system also tells Brain how your body is positioned, so you don't even have to think about it.

- ● Speed of pain signal: 98 ft. (30m) per second
- ● Visceral sensors: pick up stomachaches and other internal pains
- ● Scientific name: somatosensory system

Touch

Hormones
Body Parts

★ Moody fellows who regulate your body's functions
★ Chemical messengers that work with the nervous system
★ Produced by glands in several areas of the body

I get my name from the Greek word *horman*, meaning "to set in motion"—I make things happen. Your body functions might be all Greek to you, but without me, nothing would get done. I am produced by squishy lumps called glands, which squirt different types of me into your bloodstream. Like a messenger, I speed toward my target destination with a list of instructions. Once there, I encourage Cell to start doing things differently.

There isn't much I don't do, actually. I control the way you use energy and water. I play a role in how you sleep, and I affect your moods. One important job is reorganizing your body as it matures into an adult. That's not easy. Sometimes I overreact a little and cause a problem or two. But you get used to it; it's all part of growing up.

● Number of hormones in the body: 100
● Well-known hormones: insulin, adrenaline, testosterone, estrogen
● Largest hormone gland: thyroid

Hormones

Sperm
■ Body Parts

✳ A little squirt who wants to meet Egg
✳ Carries an X or Y chromosome to decide the sex of a baby
✳ Name is short for spermatozoon

I'm a little guy with a big job. Along with my other half, Egg, I make new life. There are no other cells like us— we can't copy ourselves and we each carry only half a set of DNA. When we meet, we fuse our half sets to make a unique genetic combo—a new human being.

I won't get anywhere unless I am fast—it's a race to reach Egg before she gets too old. And I have to be the first. I'm a champion swimmer with a long tail. My life is brief but glorious. I start out in one of the two testes, a man's sperm factories, and travel upstream toward the penis. As I pass the prostate gland, fluids get added, giving me fuel for my trip. If everything is going swimmingly, I enter a female body, and it takes an hour or so to reach Egg.

I'm made in there!

● Swimming speed: 0.04 to 0.12 in. (1 to 3mm) per minute
● Number produced per day: 50 to 500 million
● Length: 50×10^{-6}m

Sperm

Egg
■ Body Parts

☀ Sperm's life partner; together they bring babies into the world
☀ The female sex cell; its scientific name is ovum
☀ The largest cell made by the human body

I'm infinitely precious and pregnant with possibility. I'm born in a woman's ovary, and once a month I float like a miniature balloon toward her womb to make a date with Sperm—if he shows up! Men make millions of Sperm every day, but I'm much rarer. A woman will release only 400 of me in a lifetime.

I'm one big mama—85,000 times bigger than Sperm—but there is a lot more to me. I have a half set of DNA, like my male counterpart, but I also have a full team of workers such as Mitochondria and Ribosomes—everything that is needed to power my growth into a baby if I fuse with Sperm. The uterus (womb) gets ready to nurture the new life, but if Sperm doesn't arrive, I leave during a woman's monthly period.

I pop out of here!

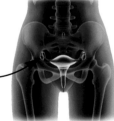

● Average size: 1.5×10^{-4} m
● Life span after release: 24 hours
● Egg + sperm = zygote

Egg

Baby in Womb
■ Body Parts

✹ This little tyke is a model of good breeding
✹ Grown from a single cell inside the womb, or uterus
✹ Supplied by a fuel pipe called the umbilical cord

I don't know much, really—I haven't even been born yet—even so, I think I might be the most amazing thing the human body can do. When Sperm and Egg get together on the way to a woman's womb, it's just the beginning of an incredible journey, one that results in a whole new person being created.

The single cell, or zygote, formed from Sperm and Egg splits in half over and over again to make a ball of cells, which glues itself to the womb. In one month I have one million cells and have formed them into two teams: one side becomes an embryo, with buds for arms, legs, and everything else. The rest is the placenta, a fueling station that supplies me with food. After nine months, I've had enough—it's time to face the world.

I'm in there!

● New babies born per year: 130 million
● Uterus size: expands to 500 times its original size
● Chances of twins: one in 70 births

Baby in Womb

Stem Cell
■ Body Parts

* A mighty morphing power cell that can grow into anything
* Found in embryos, bone marrow, the liver, and the eyes
* Could one day be used to build replacement body parts

I am the special one. I'm not like any other cell—Brain's cells are always brain cells, and Red Blood Cell can never become anything else, but I can be anything I want to be. I can grow into any type of cell I choose . . . or just keep reproducing without making a firm decision. One day I'll choose my path and grow into a liver cell, skin cell, or something else. I have so much potential!

My talents make me extremely valuable. Because I can become anything from kidney to muscle to heart cells, I could one day be used to build replacement organs. Transplants or grafts grown from me in a lab would be easy to fit. I could even be used to repair faulty DNA, which causes some of the world's most terrifying diseases such as Alzheimer's disease and Parkinson's syndrome.

● Discoverers: Ernest McCulloch and James Till (1960s)
● Where most common: growing babies in the womb
● Adult stem cells: located in bone marrow and skin

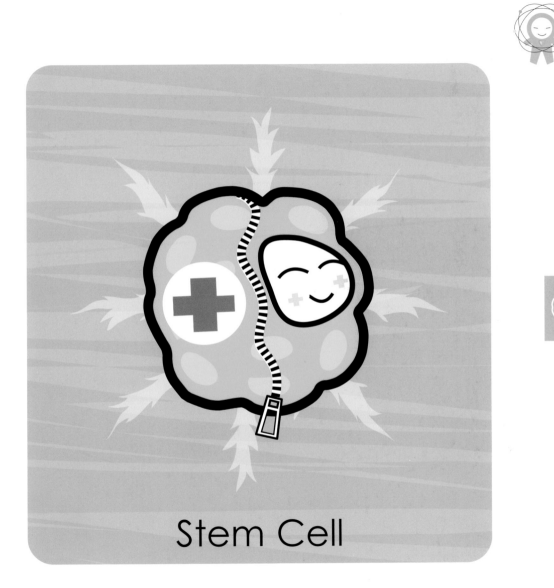

Stem Cell

Tooth
■ Body Parts

✳ A tough guy who shreds the morsels you eat
✳ This choppy fellow is a human's hardest part
✳ Needs daily brushing to scrub away nasty bacteria

Along with the body's strongest muscle—in the jaw—
and a mouthful of friends, there's not much I can't
demolish. I am built in three layers. First is a tough white
outer casing called enamel. Then comes a filler called
dentin and, finally, pulp. Your mouth is home to many
bacteria. Their waste products eat away at my enamel.
I should feel no pain because all my nerves are buried
deep down, but if bacteria break in, I'll ache for sure.

I come in four different shapes. Nippers called incisors live
at the front of the mouth. Then come canines—fangs for
stabbing food. The wide guys on each side are premolars
and molars—they bump and grind the food into a paste.
The largest molars sit at the back. You don't get these
four huge "wisdom" teeth until you are grown up.

● Number of baby teeth: 20
● Number of adult teeth: 32
● Early toothpaste: fish bones, ground lead

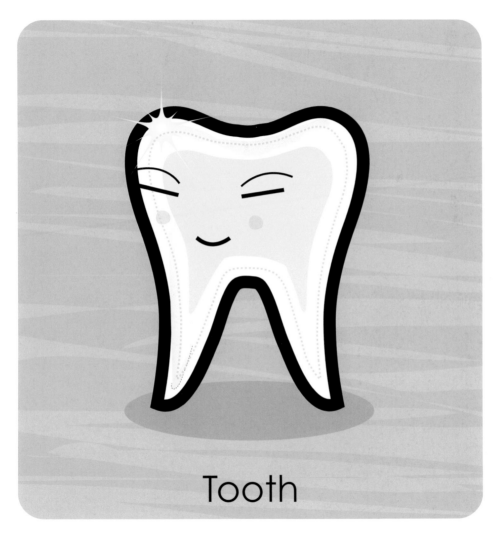

Tooth

Stomach

■ Body Parts

✳ A rotund fellow who loves a filling meal
✳ A well-muscled bag filled with acid and a few bacteria
✳ An acid bath where food breaks down

I've got a bad rep—I'm always to blame for people being too heavy. But I put up with some pretty unpleasant working conditions just to bring you the juicy goodness from the food you gobble. The juices that slosh around inside me are acidic enough to burn your skin, and I am home to an enzyme called pepsin, which breaks down proteins.

My job is to mash up your food and turn it into a thick glop called chyme. My interior is lined with a mucus layer that stops the vicious acid from burning. If that no longer works, a painful ulcer will form. I can "stomach" pretty much anything, but when something doesn't agree with me, a series of quick muscular contractions sends it back out the way it came in!

I'm back there!

● Time food is in stomach: 90 minutes to 4.5 hours
● Stomach acid: ten times stronger than vinegar
● Capacity of stomach: 1.6 qt. (1.5L)

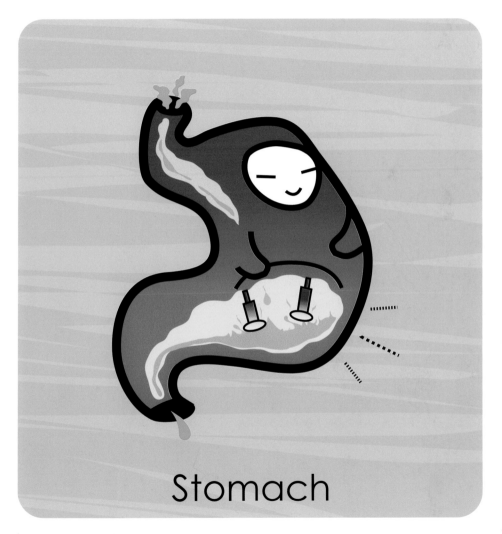

Stomach

Intestines
■ Body Parts

※ A long tube that snakes through your middle
※ Food moves through this pipe with muscular jerks and spasms
※ Nutrients from the food pass through the tube's wall into the blood

I'm a gutsy performer, the business end of your body's fabulous food-processing facility. Like a squirming serpent, I lie coiled in your belly. As churned-up grub makes its way through my long and winding loops, I use a variety of cunning tricks to suck all the best stuff from it. What's left once I've finished is smelly waste. It's the dirtiest job in the body, but someone's got to do it.

Although I'm on the inside, I'm actually an outer layer of the body—like the hole running through a very long doughnut. I have two sections. The small intestine is a narrow pipe where food is processed. Waste moves into the large intestine. The water is sucked out, leaving a stinky mixture of solids and gases, which leaves the body through the anus.

I curl up in here!

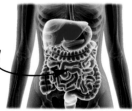

● Length of small intestine: 20 ft. (6m)
● Length of large intestine: 5 ft. (1.5m)
● Time food spends in intestines: 12 hours

Intestines

Liver
■ Body Parts

✳ A wobbly workaholic who cleans up after the rest of the body
✳ This hothouse of activity generates heat for your body
✳ Just beats Brain as the body's heaviest organ

I'm a multitasker—a jack-of-all-trades and master of every single one. If you want something done, I'm your man. With more than 500 jobs on my list, I always "de-liver"! There's so much going on inside my four floppy lobes that scientists don't know about even half of what I do.

I collect nutrients from the blood and store essential vitamins and iron. On top of that, I act like a cleaner, removing poisons as well as damaged red blood cells from your blood. I send all this waste down the line to Kidney to throw away. I'm also responsible for breaking down fat and cholesterol. Could you live without me? Well, obviously not, but you could live without 90 percent of me. I have amazing regenerative powers and can grow back from just a tiny blob.

That's me!

● Average weight: 3.1 to 3.5 lbs. (1.4 to 1.6kg)
● Proportion of body weight: two percent
● Liver diseases: hepatitis, jaundice, cirrhosis

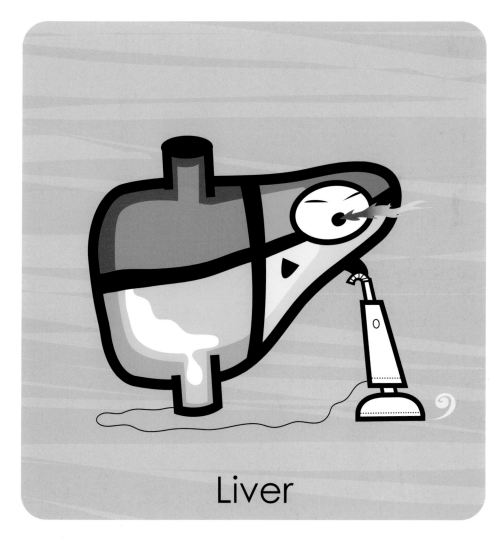

Liver

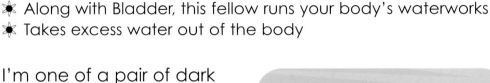

Kidney
■ Body Parts

✳ Filter that cleans the blood several times each day
✳ Along with Bladder, this fellow runs your body's waterworks
✳ Takes excess water out of the body

I'm one of a pair of dark red, bean-shaped organs that lurk in your midriff, toward the back. Although I live in a backwater, I provide an essential service. Your body creates a lot of waste every day, most of which ends up in the blood. I filter the blood and offload the waste on Bladder. Sometimes my filters get blocked with chalky stones—ouch!

Kidney

That's me, next to my partner!

● Blood processed per day: 462 gal. (1,750L)
● Urine made per day: 1.6 qt. (1.5L)
● Record number of kidney stones: 4,504

Bladder

Body Parts ■

✳ Holds your urine in an inflatable bag until it's time "to go"
✳ Urine trickles down to me from the kidneys through two tubes
✳ When full, a valve of muscle opens to release the flow

Bladder

I'm best buddies with Kidney, and together "wee" make a good team—get it? I store your urine, which is yellow because of waste from Red Blood Cell, and it's a good thing I'm not obsessed with my size, as I swell up like a balloon. When I'm full, an inner valve opens automatically. Then you'll get that urge. It's up to you to open the outer hatch when you're ready.

● Bladder capacity: 13.5 oz. (400mL)
● Urine = 96 percent water
● It's time to go to the bathroom when your bladder is half full.

I live here! ——

103

Skin

■ Body Parts

- ✳ A flexible friend who keeps you connected to the outside world
- ✳ A self-repairing fabric that responds to changing conditions
- ✳ Hot stuff that can sweat 0.5 gal. (2L) of water every hour

I am the single most advanced material known to humankind—hard wearing, waterproof, superstretchy, and extremely sensitive. I'll also keep you warm or chill you out, and I'm your first line of defense against sticks, stones, and infectious diseases. If I get bumped or gashed, I swell up to stop the threat, and blood rushes in to form a crusty barrier to the wound.

On my surface, all the cells are dead—you are always carrying around 4.4 lbs. (2kg) of dead skin—but I renew myself every month. If you get cold or frightened, my army of hairs is raised up by a team of tiny muscles—they literally give me goose bumps. Below the surface, I'm packed with sensors that can pick up pain, cold, and heat. My sweat glands cool me down, while my oil glands keep me supple.

- ● Total surface area: 20.5 sq. ft. (1.9m²)
- ● Average weight: 106 to 141 oz. (3,000 to 4,000g)
- ● Number of bacteria per square inch: more than 1.2 million (7.5 million/cm²)

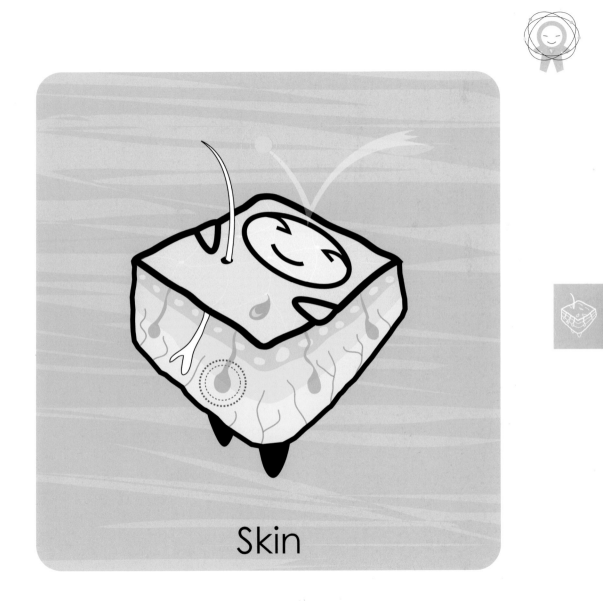

Skin

Nails

■ Body Parts

✴ Hard-bitten guys growing at the ends of your fingers and toes
✴ Sharp-suited characters made from the protein keratin
✴ Despite the rumors, nails don't keep growing after you die

Built to scratch, pinch, and gouge, we're some of the toughest guys in the body. But owing to our brittle personalities, we usually crack under pressure. Made from the same stuff as gorgeous Hair, we're her rough little brothers and are as hard as, well, nails. We may be tough, but we like to look our best. Keep us trim and nicely shaped—but remember, don't bite!

Nails

● Growth rate: 0.12 in. (3mm) per month
● Longest fingernails: 24.6 ft. (7.51m)
● Animals with nails: all primates

Hair
Body Parts

* Curly, wavy, or straight lengths made of keratin
* Grows out of hair follicles embedded in the skin
* Stronger than a copper wire of the same thickness

Hair

I grow mostly on the head to keep it warm—it can get cold up there without me. But you can find me almost everywhere—not just in the shower drain, but all over the rest of your body, except your lips, palms, and the soles of your feet. Half of you try to get rid of me wherever I crop up, while the other half unhappily count every strand of me that falls from your heads.

● Number of hairs on head: 90,000 to 150,000
● Growth rate: 0.39 in. (1cm) per month
● Longest-ever hair: 18.5 ft. (5.63m)

CHAPTER 4
Green Shoots

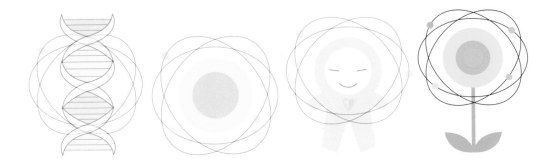

This gang of green friends is intimately involved in the private life of almost everything alive on this planet. More than 90 percent of the 75 billion tons of living things on Earth is greenery. These veggies are the silent heroes of life. They do all the hard work of capturing the Sun's energy and turning it into food. Without them, animals and other living things would have nothing to eat. The green team also floods the air with life-giving oxygen for us to breathe. All plants, such as ferns, fir trees, and flowers, are made out of the same type of plant cells, but some of this clean-cut crew are found only in flowering plants.

Plant Cell

Chlorophyll

Leaf

Stem

Root

Flower

Pollen

Seed

Fruit

Plant Cell
Green Shoots

☀ An all-action hero who runs the show inside plants
☀ All plant parts are made from this mighty, mini building block
☀ Water is crammed inside to make this guy a really solid fellow

I am nothing less than the hub of all plant life on Earth. A versatile all-arounder, my all-purpose body is equipped to build all the parts that a plant needs. I may be a tiny tot, but I keep myself in shape—usually a solidly built box with stiff cell walls. This allows me to stack together in many different shapes, and because I can split myself in half, it's easy for plants to grow new parts.

My secret is that I am crammed with all sorts of useful odds and ends called organelles. These top-class troops make plants tick. Chloroplasts, for example, are chock-full of Chlorophyll for converting the Sun's energy; Mitochondria provide the power; the nucleus coordinates the activity. But I'm literally a sap—there's a big sac, or vacuole, in my middle, and it's full of juicy sap!

● Discoverer: Robert Hooke (1665)
● Average size: 10 to 100×10^{-6}m
● Types of plant cells include: leaf, stem, root

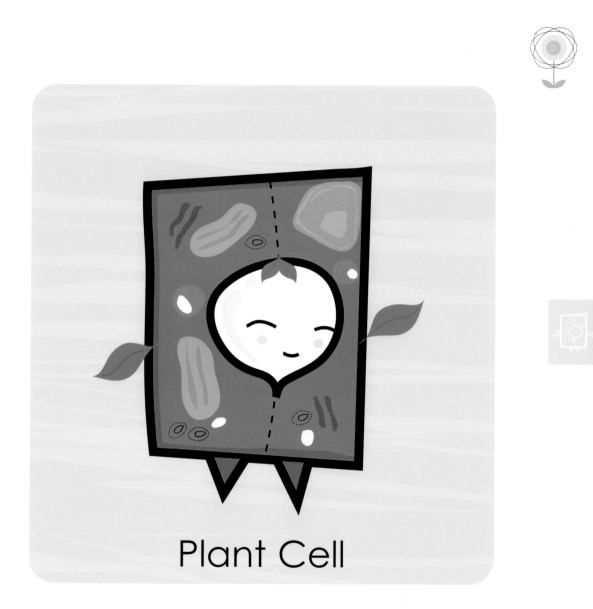

Plant Cell

Chlorophyll
■ Green Shoots

* ✹ The green stuff that makes life on Earth possible
* ✹ Found in chloroplasts inside plant cells
* ✹ Uses sunlight to make sugary plant food by photosynthesis

I'm a miracle molecule who's fantastic at absorbing light. My talent might even make me the single most important chemical on the planet. I drink in energy from the Sun and use it to power the production of sugar—food for a plant and ultimately for all things on Earth, too. As if that wasn't enough, this process (called photosynthesis) also produces the oxygen that all animals breathe and sucks up that nasty greenhouse gas carbon dioxide.

I put the "green" in greenery. I live inside chloroplasts, tiny little green blobs rammed inside the cells of Leaf. Because I absorb blue and red light but not green— which is reflected back—I give plants their color. In the fall, many plants get rid of me, and their leaves turn a golden yellow color.

* ● Discoverer: Hans Fischer (1940)
* ● Number of versions of chlorophyll: six
* ● Number of chloroplasts that would fit on a period: 10,000

Chlorophyll

Leaf
Green Shoots

- ✳ A Sun-loving lounger that collects the energy used by plants
- ✳ Has been growing on plants for at least 400 million years
- ✳ Usually flat and wide to help catch the Sun's rays

It's a tough life being a leaf. My job is to bask in the sunshine all day long, soaking up as much light as I can. Ah! Sounds like bliss, but I'm no slouch. I make all the food for a plant.

I'm more organized than you might think. I'm positioned so that I don't block out the light for other leaves, and I can't be too heavy, so I have a superlight internal skeleton.

I also do the "breathing" for a plant, absorbing carbon dioxide through tiny pores on my surface. I often have a waxy coating to stop me from losing water. Because I'm full of sugar, I make a tasty treat for creatures such as sheep, insects, and humans, so I sometimes defend myself with poisons or stinging spines. You're not the only one who hates hearing the words "Eat your greens!"

- ● Largest leaves: a type of raffia palm, *Raffia regalis* (79 ft./24m long)
- ● Leaves per tree (oak): 200,000
- ● Leaf weight (oak): 1.6 tons over 60 years

Leaf

Stem

■ Green Shoots

☀ This upstanding guy uses cellulose to stiffen plant-cell walls
☀ Always on hand to make sure nothing droops
☀ A sucker who helps transport a plant's liquid lunch

I'm a stiff sort of fellow who gets the thirsty work done for plants. I take water to Leaf and his friends and deliver food in the form of syrupy sap. The plant cells I use are harder than most, with woody walls that make excellent tubes for slurping up liquid and making a plant stand at attention. Unfortunately, this stiff stuff also makes vegetables stringy.

Stem

● First plant with stems: fern
● Longest stem (redwood): 367 ft. (112m)
● Edible stems include: celery, rhubarb

Root
Green Shoots

✳ First thing a new plant does is put down roots
✳ These hairy suckers get all the best stuff out of the ground
✳ Evaporation from leaves pulls water up through a plant

Root

Shy, retiring, and very down-to-earth, I prefer to bury myself in my work and not show my face. Doing the grunt work, I take up water and essential minerals from the soil and provide a solid base for future growth. I also store any spare starch and sugar in bulbous underground tubers, such as potatoes, carrots, and turnips, which humans love to dig up and eat.

● Deepest root: 197 ft. (60m) (in Arizona)
● Edible roots include: yams, ginger
● First root to grow from a seed: radicle

Flower

▪ Green Shoots

- ✱ Flowering plants use this blooming beauty to spread pollen
- ✱ Collects pollen from other flowers using a sticky stigma
- ✱ If fertilized by pollen, the ovary swells into fruit with seeds inside

Reproductive and seductive, I'm a temptress with one thing on my mind—to spread copies of myself far and wide. I come clothed in the loveliest of colors, with a fiendish array of love traps, perfumes, and sweet, sweet nectar to lure insects, birds, and even bats to help me complete my mission. Humans use me as a token of love. I'm so beautiful that I'm scientifically proven to make people smile.

As well as my petals, I also have male parts called stamens, which produce pollen, and a female part called a pistil (made of a stigma and an ovary). A pollen cell from another flower tunnels into the pistil to reach an ovule inside my ovary. The two combine to make Seed. Then my pretty parts die, and my leftovers grow into Fruit.

- ● Largest flower: *Rafflesia arnoldii* (3.3 ft./1m)
- ● *Rafflesia* flower weight: 24 lbs. (11kg)
- ● *Rafflesia* scent: rotting flesh

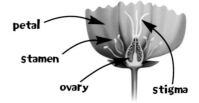

petal
stamen
ovary
stigma

Flower

Pollen

Green Shoots

✸ Golden dust that fertilizes a flower's ovule
✸ Made by the male parts of flowers and causes hay fever
✸ Eaten by bees and other insects

Tough and intrepid, I'm all man. My mission is to find the female parts of plants of my species and fertilize them to make Seed. But I get up the noses of some people and even make them cry. Let me set the record straight.

One way of getting around, if you are microscopically small like me, is to be blown around in the air. It's not funny for hay-fever sufferers! Insects visiting flowers for nectar get me stuck on their legs, and I end up on the gooey tip of a pistil. Then my coat cracks open, and I drill into the ovary to help make Seed. My outer coat is so tough that I can last for thousands of years. Archaeologists use me to find out what plants prehistoric people used. Because my spiky coat sticks to clothing, I can also be used to place the bad guys at the scene of a crime.

I'm aiming for here!

I'm made here!

● Number of grains per flower: around 7,000
● Pollen causing hay fever: grass, oil-seed rape, birch
● Maximum distance traveled: 3,000 mi. (4,800km)

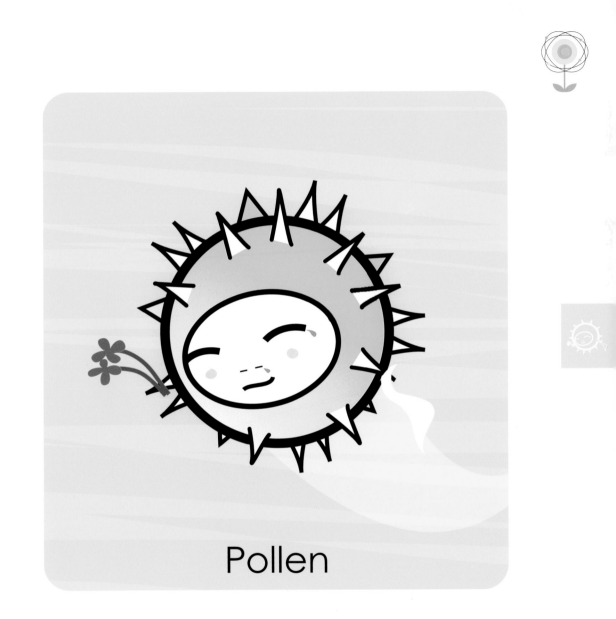

Pollen

Seed

Green Shoots

* A tough nut made inside the center of flowers
* Used by plants to grow new copies of themselves
* Clothed in a resilient jacket and built to last for years

I am the great hope—
a package that contains
everything needed to
make a new plant, sent
out to colonize Earth. I'm
tough and can survive
without food, water, or
air for hundreds of years.
I am scattered in the wind
or hitch a ride on animal
hairs with my Velcrolike
hooks. Often I get eaten
as part of Fruit and
slip through an animal's
guts onto the ground.

Seed

● Number of seeds per plant: 10 to 100,000
● Largest seed: coco-de-mer (44 lbs./20kg)
● Longest-lived seed: lotus (700 years)

Fruit
Green Shoots

* Sweet, savory, or sour treat made by flowering plants
* Mostly, the flower's ovary forms the fruit, enclosing the seeds
* This ripe fellow moves seeds far away from the parents

Fruit

Don't mix me up with vile vegetables—I'm much sweeter. I'm the plump and juicy flesh that surrounds Seed. That's why tomatoes and cucumbers are fruit. I am often full of sugar and make a delicious snack (healthy, too!). I don't mind getting eaten—in fact, that's the point. Being swallowed makes sure that Seed ends up a long way from his parent plant.

● Heaviest fruit: pumpkin (995 lbs./450kg)
● Deadliest fruit: castor bean, source of the poison ricin
● Unusual fruit: mangosteen, ugli fruit, durian

INDEX

GLOSSARY

Alveoli Tiny sacs in the lungs where oxygen passes from the air into the blood.

Antibody A chemical tag that is made by cells in the immune system such as B cells. Antibodies stick to viruses and bacteria that invade the body. The antibodies mark the invaders for destruction by T cells.

ATP Short for adenosine triphosphate, the chemical used to store energy in cells.

Carbon dioxide An invisible gas made from carbon and oxygen atoms. Carbon dioxide is a waste product made by living things as they burn their food fuel. Plants also use carbon-dioxide gas to make sugar.

Cartilage A tough, flexible tissue; also known as gristle. Sharks' skeletons are made out of cartilage.

Chloroplast An organelle found in most plant cells where photosynthesis takes place.

Chromosome A structure in a cell nucleus that holds a fragile DNA molecule. Human cells have 46 chromosomes, but that number varies from species to species.

Cilia Tiny structures that stick out of the sides of a cell and drift like hairs. Cilia are used to collect food, sense movement, and push a cell along.

Fertilize When two sex cells, such as a sperm and an egg, fuse together to make an embryo that will develop into a new plant or animal.

Gland A group of cells that releases a substance, such as a hormone, into or onto the body.

Immune system The body's protection system, which keeps it free from disease. Its cells

clean out any invaders such as bacteria and viruses.

Kingdom The largest grouping used to categorize different types of organisms. There are five kingdoms: plants, animals, fungi, protists, and bacteria.

Lymphatic system A body group that removes a greenish liquid that builds up in the muscles. The liquid, called lymph, drains through a network of vessels. Any viruses or bacteria are filtered out at lymph nodes before the lymph is dripped slowly back into the blood.

Metabolism The word used to describe all of a body's processes.

Molecule The smallest possible unit of a chemical. If a molecule is broken down into smaller sections, it will no longer be the same chemical.

Nucleus An area in the center of most types of cells where DNA is coiled up on chromosomes.

Organ A structure in the body that performs several roles. The largest organ in the human body is the liver. Others include the lungs, heart, and brain.

Organelle A tiny structure inside the cells of plants, animals, fungi, and protists that performs a certain job. Mitochondria and chloroplasts are organelles.

Oxygen An invisible gas that is mixed with other gases in the air. Living things take oxygen from the air to burn the fuel in their food in order to power their bodies.

Photosynthesis The process used by plants and some bacteria and protists to turn carbon dioxide and water into sugar using the energy in sunlight. Oxygen is released as a waste product.

GLOSSARY

Protein One of a group of substances that help build and run cells. Each type of protein has a certain shape, which controls the way it works. All enzymes and some hormones are made of proteins.

Protist One of a kingdom of organisms that normally have bodies made from only one cell. Protist cells are larger and more complicated than those of bacteria and are structured more like animal, fungus, and plant cells.

Species A group of living things that look the same and can breed with one another. For example, lions form a species, as do apples and button mushrooms.

Stamen The male part of a flower where pollen is produced.

Stigma A sticky tip on a flower where pollen from another flower is collected.

System A group of organs and tissues associated with a particular body function that interact with one another. For example, the liver, stomach, and intestines are some of the organs that work together in the digestive system.

Urine A liquid waste produced by vertebrates as their kidneys clean their blood.

Vacuole A sac of liquid in the center of a plant cell. The sac is used as a supply of water.

Vertebrate An animal that has a backbone, or spine. Fish, amphibians, reptiles, birds, and mammals are all vertebrates.

Zygote The first cell of a new living thing formed by fertilization. The zygote eventually grows into a full body.